Spiritual Truth Series

Volume 1

The Gifts, Grace and Flow of the Holy Spirit

Understanding Guide

Brenda St. John
in connection with
Jan Coverstone

Spiritual

Truth Series

Volume 1: The Gifts, Grace and Flow of the Holy Spirit

Understanding Guide

By Brenda St. John

in connection with

Jan Coverstone

Copyright 2018 by Jan Coverstone

Scripture taken from the New King James Version. Copyright 1982 by Thomas Nelson Inc. Used by permission. All rights reserved.

Published by JC Life Books Columbia City, Indiana USA

www.jancoverstone.com

With special thanks to the Fellowship Group of Columbia City Christian Fellowship Church for using their study time to evaluate this workbook; and for their comments and suggestions for improvements to enhance your learning experience. We all would love to help you grow in your understanding of the Holy Spirit and become supernaturally normal in your Christian life for the benefit of all those God has connected to you during this time on Earth. Blessings.

I have discovered that a strong key to understand the scriptures is understanding the differences in word usage from Bibles times until now. Mr. Coverstone does in depth research to find the meanings to words that God chose to have written. Often word's meanings have evolved to something different and cause us to see the intent or situation written about differently. These clear explanations have provided me greater understanding to be able to grow in my walk.

Ch. 1 Personal Experience

First let's review the events of the author's story.

He talked to God as a child.

He refused to follow God as a teenager.

In a life threatening situation he asked God to help him saying that he would try to follow God.

He recovered. Questions began filling his head.

He felt the warmth of God.

God spoke audibly to him and they conversed about many of his questions.

His disposition improved and he actually felt like smiling.

He went to church and prayed and was slain in the spirit.

He received the Holy Spirit, spoke in tongues and danced in the spirit.

He began witnessing to others about his experience.

Next let's think about and discuss chapter 1.

1. Does this experience raise doubts or faith in you? _____
Explain_____

_____

_____

_____

2. Is God still able to do miracles?

_____

_____

_____

_____

3. Have you experienced miracles and/or extraordinary experiences in your life?

_____

_____

_____

_____

4. Do you think you would be different if you had a similar life story?

_____

_____

_____

ACTIVATION EXERCISE: imagine you are hearing the voice of the Lord. What would He say to you? If the Lord physically moved you (lifted you from your seat) how would that change your perspective?

Ch. 2 The Promise of the Spirit

First let's remind ourselves of the referenced scriptures.

I indeed baptize you with _____ unto _____, but He who is coming after me is mightier than I, whose sandals I am not worthy to carry. He will baptize you with the _____ and _____.
(Mt. 3:11)

And he preached, saying, "There comes One after me who is mightier than I, whose sandal strap I am not worthy to stoop down and loose. I indeed _____ you with _____, but He will _____ you with _____.
(Mk. 1:7-8) John answered, saying to all, *"I indeed _____ you with _____, but one _____ than I is coming, whose sandal strap I am not worthy to loose. He will _____ you with the _____ and with _____.* (Lk 3:16)

And John bore witness, saying, "I saw the _____ descending from _____ like a _____ and He remained upon Him. I did not know Him, but He who sent me to baptize with water said to me, 'Upon whom you see the _____ descending, and remaining on Him, this is He who _____ with the _____.' And I have seen and testified that this is the _____ of God." (Jn. 1:23-24)

"If a son asks for bread from any father among you will he give him a stone? Or if he asks for a fish, will be give him a serpent instead of a fish? Or if he asks for an egg, will he offer him a scorpion? If you then, being evil, know how to give _____ gifts to your _____, how much more will your heavenly _____ give the _____ to those who _____ Him!" (Lk 11:11-13)

"On the last day, that great day of the feast, Jesus stood and cried out. Saying, "If anyone _____ let him come to Me and drink. He who believes in Me, as the Scripture has said, out of his heart will flow rivers of _____."

But this He spoke concerning the _____ whom those _____ in Him would _____; for the Holy Spirit was not yet given because Jesus was not yet glorified. (Jn. 7:37-39)

"And I will pray the Father and He will give you another _____, that He may abide with you _____ — The _____ of truth, whom the world cannot receive, because it neither sees Him nor knows Him; but you know Him, for He dwells with you and will be in you. (Jn. 14:16-17) But the Helper, the _____ whom the _____ will send in _____ name, He will _____ you all things, and bring to your _____ all things that I said to you. (Jn. 14:26)

"Behold. I send the _____ of My Father upon you; but _____ in the city of Jerusalem until you are endued with _____ from on high." (Lk.24:49

And being assembled together with them, He commanded them _____ to depart from Jerusalem, but to _____ for _____ of the Father, "which," He said, "you have heard from Me; for _____ truly baptized with _____, but you shall be baptized with the _____ not many days from now." Therefore, when they had come together, they asked Him, saying, "Lord, will You at this time restore the kingdom to Israel?" And He said to them, "It is not for you to know times or seasons which the Father has put in His own Authority. But you shall receive _____ when the _____ has come upon _____; and you shall be _____ to Me in Jerusalem, and in all Judea and Samaria, and to the _____ of the earth." (Acts. 1:4-8)

When the day of Pentecost had fully come, they were all with one accord in one place. And suddenly there came a sound from _____, as of a rushing mighty _____, and it filled the whole house where they were sitting. Then there appeared to them divided _____, as of _____, and one sat upon _____ of them. And they were _____ filled with the

7

_____ *and began to* _____ *with other tongues, as the* _____ *gave them utterance.* (Acts 2:1-4)

But Peter, standing up with the eleven, raised his voice and said to them, "Men of Judea and all who dwell in Jerusalem, let this be known to you, and heed my words. For these are not drunk, as you suppose, since it is only the third hour of the day. But this is what was _____ *by the prophet Joel: And it shall come to pass in the last days, says God, That I will pour out My* _____ *on* _____ *flesh; your sons and daughters shall* _____, *your young men shall see* _____, *your old men shall dream* _____, *And on My menservants and on My maidservants I will pour out* _____ *Spirit in those days; and they shall* _____. (Acts 2:14-18)

The word _____ comes from different Greek words. *Exousia* has the meaning privilege, force, capacity, competence, freedom, token of control authority, jurisdiction, liberty, power, right or strength: it is translated in newer versions as authority. *Dunamis* means force, miraculous power, abundance, ability, might, worker of miracles, power strength, or mighty work. The _____ Jesus was talking about which came on the Day of Pentecost was not given to the _____ only but to _____ who _____ the _____ of the _____. *Dunamis* is the root word for dynamite and *dyne* which is a unit of work. The power was given to have some dynamite; to have explosive power for the

_____, _____, _____ and being a _____ for Christ.

Next let's think about and discuss the passages of truth taken from the referenced Scriptures concerning the Holy Spirit. What does each of these truths mean to you?

John the Baptist foretold of one greater than himself who would baptize with the Holy Spirit and fire.

1. Who did John refer to? _____

2. Why are there two different baptisms?

_____

_____

_____

When the Holy Spirit abode on Christ it signified He would baptize you with the Holy Spirit and fire.

3. Why did the dove descend on Jesus?

_____

Christ said the Father would give the Holy Spirit to those who ask.

4. Whom did Jesus say God felt was important enough to receive the Holy Spirit? _____

Christ said if anyone would thirst and come to Him and out of His belly (innermost being, spirit) would flow rivers of living water.

5. How does the analogy of thirst and flowing rivers explain the mission of the Holy Spirit?

_____

_____

The Holy Spirit is to be a comforter and the Promise of the Father.

6. How does this make you feel? Why would someone not want the Holy Spirit in their life?

_____

_____

_____

The Holy Spirit endues with power.

7. What is the purpose of the power the Holy Spirit provides?

_____

_____

_____

_____

It was so vital Christ commanded His disciples to tarry in Jerusalem until they were endued with power.

8. What might have happened with the disciples if they had not waited for the power of the Holy Spirit?

_____

_____

_____

_____

9. What effect came from the believers all being in one place on the day of Pentecost?

_____

_____

_____

_____

The Holy Spirit came with the sound of a mighty rushing wind and cloven tongues of fire which sat upon each of them.

10. Why didn't God just deliver the Holy Spirit quietly and calmly?

_____

_____

_____

All the one hundred and twenty received the Holy Spirit and all spoke with tongues as the Spirit gave them utterance.

11. Who spoke through the believers at Pentecost? _____

12. Should we also have a time of waiting or seeking the same promise of the Father? _____

_____

13. Peter seemed clear and confident when he spoke to the crowd. How do you think you would have reacted in this situation?

_____

_____

14. Do you view the help of the Holy Spirit as positive or negative? _____ Why? _____

_____

_____

15. If all believers today were taught, comforted and empowered by the Holy Spirit how might the world be different?

_____

_____

_____

Ch. 3 The Baptism in the Holy Spirit

First let's remind ourselves of the information presented in Ch. 3.

There were two physical evidences of the coming of the Holy Spirit into the disciples and followers of Jesus in the upper room in Jerusalem on the Day of Pentecost.

(1) Sound from heaven as of _____ and (2) visually divided tongues as of _____

The word for _____, in the Hebrew, is *ruwach* which is translated _____ from the root of the same word which means to blow, i.e. breathe. The word in the Greek is the word *pneuma* which is a _____, breath or a breeze and by analogy a spirit, Christ's Spirit or the Holy Spirit.

The Angel of the Lord appeared to him in a _____ from the midst of a bush. (Exodus 3:2) When the nation of Israel left Egypt the Lord went before them by day in a pillar of cloud to lead the way and by night in a _____ to give them light, so as to go by day and night. (Exodus 13:21)

The experience of receiving the _____ and speaking with other _____ came with the presence of wind and the anointing of fire. There was no doubt this was the presence and movement of the _____.

The Scriptures give description and explanation of what occurred on the Day of Pentecost.

And they were _____ _____ with the Holy Spirit and began to _____ with other tongues, as the Spirit _____ them utterance. (Acts 2:1-4)

It might have sounded like a tornado but was _____ enough to gather a _____.

These were people from every _____ under heaven. They heard them speak in their own _____. At least sixteen regions or cultures are mentioned and each heard their native tongue being spoken and telling of the wonderful works of _____.

When Peter stood and spoke to the multitude who gathered to _____ the pouring forth of the Holy Spirit and speaking with tongues he concluded by saying; "Repent and let every one of you be _____ in the name of _____ for the remission of sins; and you shall _____ the gift of the _____. For the _____ is to _____ and to your _____ and to _____ who are _____ off, as many as the _____ our God will call." (Acts 2:38-39)

Explanation of types of prayers

Paul stated *he would pray with the _____ and pray with the _____ and he would sing in or with the spirit and also sing with the understanding.* (I Cor. 14:14-15) When one speaks, prays or sings with the spirit the _____ in a person is using the _____ _____ to speak but it does _____ go through the _____ and _____. There is no understanding as to what is being brought forth.

Some examples of the importance of the baptism of the Holy Spirit

Acts chapter three relates the story of _____ a lame man who had never walked. It was the _____ of the Holy Spirit demonstrated and _____ in five thousand _____ in the Lord.

One aspect of the Baptism of the Holy Spirit is a greater
_____ and _____ to expound on the things
of _____ even to the _____ it amazes others.

*And Stephen, full of _____ and _____ (dunamis), did
great _____ and _____ among the people.*
(Acts 6:8) *And they were not able to resist the _____
and the _____ by which he spoke.* (Acts 6:10) Stephen
was a _____ not an apostle. He was _____
in what he was given to do and the Lord _____ his
ministry. Philip, another deacon went to Samaria and preached
and _____ multitudes and they saw the
_____, the deliverances and _____.

Peter and Cornelius both received an instructional
_____ which brought Peter to the house of Cornelius.
*"And the following day they entered Caesarea. Now Cornelius
was waiting for them and had called together his relatives and
close friends...While Peter was still speaking these words, the
Holy Spirit _____ _____ those who _____ the
_____. And those of the circumcision who believed were
astonished, as many as came with Peter, because the _____
of the Holy Spirit had been poured out on the
_____ also. For they heard them speak with
_____ and _____ God. Then Peter
answered, "Can anyone forbid water, that these should not be
baptized who have received the Holy Spirit just as we have?"*
(Acts 10:24, 44-47)

Next let's think about and discuss the Baptism of the Holy Spirit.

1. In Chapter 2 We discussed this question. Now with a greater
understanding of the mighty rushing wind and tongues of fire and the
crowd that gathered answer this question again. Why didn't God just

deliver the Holy Spirit quietly and calmly?

_____

_____

_____

2. The passages from the book of The Acts of the Apostles show the experiences of being baptized with or in the Holy Spirit were normal for the church. Is it still or should it be normal in our experience today?_____

_____

_____

3. There are many examples of the power of the Holy Spirit in the scriptures. Why would Jesus and God want us to have this power and how can we be more effective with it? _____

_____

_____

4. What influences might have stopped Christians from accepting the baptism of the Holy Spirit?

_____

_____

5. Does your spirit pray and sing in the spirit (with tongues)? What is stopping you?

_____

_____

ACTIVATION EXERCISE: If you have not received this blessing are you willing to open yourself to it? Have you led others to this experience? Why or Why not? Do these chapters help you in telling others?

Ch. 4 Reasons to Pray in Tongues

First let's remind ourselves of the information presented in Ch. 4.

These reasons for praying in tongues can be determined from the scriptures sited in the book.

(1) Tongues are an indication of the supernatural power of the Holy Spirit indwelling believers.

(2) When you receive the Holy Spirit you are also receiving the power to be witnesses to Christ.

(3) Speaking with tongues are a fulfillment of prophecy. It also helps in your spiritual growth.

(4) Praying in the spirit is a rest and refreshing.

(5) When we speak in a tongue we are speaking to God and things which were unknown are now becoming known.

(6) Speaking in a tongue builds a spiritual foundation for your life.

(7) It is the desire of the Father, the Lord Jesus, the Holy Spirit and the apostle Paul that all would speak in tongues.

(8) Using a tongue with interpretation to bring a blessing from the loving heart of the Father to those who gather together.

(9) Praying in tongues opens a new frontier to worship and magnify God.

(10) Being obedient and singing in the Spirit may bring great blessings to those around us.

(11) Interceding on the behalf of others is one of the usages of a tongue or prayer language.

(12) Praying in the Spirit is a weapon to fight a spiritual battle.

(13) Praying in the Holy Spirit builds our faith and helps keep us in the love of God.

(14) We yield ourselves to the anointing, unction, or leading of the Holy Spirit and cooperate with Him but our spirits are under our control.

(15) The beauty and majesty of the Holy Spirit's moving unites and brings a group, fellowship or local assembly closer to the Lord Jesus Christ.

Next let's think about and discuss the Reasons to Pray in Tongues.

1. Points 1, 2, and 3 above refer to our furtherment of authority to witness for Christ. Are we able to witness without the supernatural power of the Holy Spirit that Jesus told his followers to wait for? How will our witness be different if we are empowered by the Holy Spirit?

_____

_____

_____

_____

2. The underlying reason for half of the scriptures referred to (points 3, 4, 6, 8, 10, 13, & 15 above) has one theme. What is that purpose? And why would a believer not want the baptism of the Holy Spirit and ability to speak in tongues with this understanding?

_____

_____

_____

_____

3. Spiritual warfare, intercession and understanding are an important benefit of praying in tongues as mentioned in points 5, 11, & 12. Why would the Holy Spirit want to reveal knowledge and assist us in these endeavors? And why would not just anybody be privy to information the Spirit could reveal about others?

_____

_____

_____

_____

4. Specifically 7, 8, 9, 13, 14, & 15 are about our connection with God and His desire that we can communicate with Him in a prayer language specifically understood by Him. How can this be a benefit?

_____

_____

_____

5. Have any of these reasons changed your thinking about praying in tongues? _____

_____

Activation Exercise: If the group is large enough to have individuals practice sharing the reasons to pray in the spirit: let one person share the reasons and others ask questions as though they didn't believe. Each person should take a turn sharing the reasons to pray in the spirit so all may become stronger in their confidence to share.

Ch. 5 The Trinity Gives Gifts

First let's remind ourselves of the information presented in Ch. 5.

The gifts of God to the church are activities for use within the body of believers: prophecy, ministry, teaching, exhortation, giving, leadership, mercy, helps and administration.

The gifts (doma) of Christ to the church are people who are anointed to minister to others for the growth of the body of Christ: apostles, prophets, evangelists, pastors and teachers.

The spirituals (gifts) (charisma) of the Holy Spirit to the church are a divine enablement, endowment or miraculous faculty: manifestation of the Spirit, word of wisdom, word of knowledge, faith, healings, working of miracles, prophecy, discerning of spirits, different kinds of tongues, and interpretation of tongues.

All the spirituals are the best gifts. The best gifts at any time are what the Holy Spirit knows is needed for that particular situation.

We cannot force or make the spirituals operate in our lives but we learn to present ourselves as open vessels through which the power of the spirituals may flow.

In that first verse of 1 Corinthians chapter 12 Paul stated he did not want us to be ignorant. Paul wanted the church to have knowledge and understanding of this aspect of the Holy Spirit's power ministry and how these should function and flow in the body of Christ.

Paul said to earnestly desire the best gifts. He also said pursue love and desire spirituals but especially that you may prophesy. Since, they were zealous for spirituals let it be for the edification of the church. We should have an intense desire for the operation or manifestation of the spirituals in our lives. The Holy Spirit can only work through us if we desire to be used.

Love should be the guiding factor for the manifestations of the Holy Spirit as explained in 1Cor Ch. 13.

We should also conclude it was a manifestation of God's love flowing through the Holy Spirit abiding on Christ to touch those lives and bring them to believe in the Lord.

It is exciting to know the love of the Father will flow into someone's life because I desire the spirituals and allow myself to be a willing vessel for their operation.

To desire the spirituals and to be used by the Holy Spirit is to have passion and compassion to see the love of God poured into people's lives so they will accept the love gift of God's Son and have their lives forever changed to become followers of Christ.

Next let's think about and discuss the Gifts of the Trinity.

1. What would be the purpose of the Trinity giving different types of gifts and not all just randomly giving any of the gifts?

_____

_____

_____

2. Are one set of the Trinity's gifts any more or less important than the others? Why do you believe this?

_____

_____

_____

3. Are any of the spirituals more important or valuable? Why might some Christians believe that some of them are unimportant for today and we should not allow the Holy Spirit to use us in that way? _____

_____

_____

_____

_____

4. What should be our driving force in accessing the spirituals and subsequently the usage of them?

_____

_____

_____

ACTIVATION EXERCISE: Is there any who needs prayer and/or an assurance of the love of the Father? To share the Love of the Father is the most important aspect of the spirituals!!! Before praying for one another ask the Holy Spirit to guide you and love that person.

Ch. 6 Vocal Gifts

First let's remind ourselves of the information presented in Ch. 6.

"..to another the working of miracles, to another prophecy, to another discerning of spirits, to another different kinds of tongues, to another the interpretation of tongues." (1 Cor. 12:10) "Pursue _____, and _____ spiritual gifts, but _____ that you may _____. For he who speaks in a _____ does not speak to men but to _____, for no one understands him; however in the _____ he speaks mysteries. But he who _____ speaks edification and exhortation and comfort to men. He who speaks in a tongue edifies himself, but he who prophesies edifies the church. I wish _____ _____ spoke with tongues, but even _____ that you prophesied; for he who prophesies is greater than he who speaks with tongues, unless he interprets, that the church may receive edification." (1 Cor. 14:1-5)

"How is it then brethren? Whenever you come together, _____ of _____ has a psalm, has a teaching, has a tongue, has a revelation, has an interpretation. Let _____ things be done for _____." (1 Cor. 14:26)

"Therefore tongues are for a _____, not to those who believe but to _____: but prophesying is not for unbelievers but for those who _____. Therefore if the whole church comes together in one place, and all speak with tongues, and there come in those who are uninformed or unbelievers, will they not say that you are out of your mind? But if all prophesy, and an unbeliever or an uninformed person comes in, he is convinced by all, he is convicted by all. And thus the secrets of his heart are revealed; and so falling down on his face, he will worship God and report that _____ is truly _____ you." (1 Cor. 14:22-25)

Tongues and their interpretation equals _____. To prophesy is to speak to men to edify, exhort and comfort. Remember we are in the arena of manifesting the _____ given and directed by the _____. When the Holy Spirit is using a person in this manner they are bringing to the assembly a _____ to build, encourage or comfort from the Heavenly throne room. It becomes a _____ message from the loving throne of the _____ brought into the physical realm by cooperation with and yielding to the Holy Spirit.

The way spirituals are manifested is by _____ with and _____ to the Holy Spirit. You may feel a gentle leading. You may sense an urge to speak. You may become nervous and feel as though you are on fire. How you are personally led by the Holy Spirit may be unique to you. You may feel a stirring or bubbling from within you which continues until you speak forth. You may see the color green and to you it means to go with a prophecy. Our walk with the Lord is by _____, yielding and being sensitive to Him. It is the same with the _____ of the spirituals. It is yielding to the Holy Spirit. There is not a handbook to reveal how the Holy Spirit will move in and through you. But rest assured all can prophesy; that is a _____ from God.

All the manifestations are from God through the _____ and flow from the throne room of _____. This will _____prophecies which are judgmental, which have personal directives or are from a person who just erred in the delivery. If it does not edify, exhort and comfort _____ about it and decide if you should keep it or discard it. All should be done in _____, grace and mercy with tenderness and _____.

How do you function with or flow in the grace of the spirituals? Read and study and _____ the Holy Spirit to guide and teach you. He came to be a _____ and to _____ and lead us into all truth. _____ in the spirit will help your

_____ to the leading and outflow of other gifts. Prophecy may bring forth a word of _____ or word of _____ as you are speaking. By being sensitive and yielding to the Holy Spirit, the other spirituals follow prayer and or prophecy.

Our Father desires to _____ to us. The Holy Spirit is waiting for us to _____ His manifestation so the _____ of the Father and our Lord Jesus Christ may flow and bless the church.

Commentary by Brenda.

Much of this chapter relates to that which we call a church service. As with most every aspect of life, changes occur over time and the way an event took place a few generations ago can be very different than it happens now. Example the Thanksgiving feast in 1621 w the pilgrims and the Indians changed drastically through time and now our lifestyle does not even consist of wild game and over the fire cooking. We do not have similar situations to survive through. Our work is extremely different. We relate to family and friends completely different. Our homes and lives currently leave children to believe that event was a "fairy tale," almost beyond their imagination.

When reading about the early church in Acts, and even reading the letters of Paul to later churches, people of this time have a difficult time relating to how their "services" would have been conducted. It describes them more as in home prayer meetings, or outdoor gatherings. In Acts many of the believers in the upper room were followers of Jesus who would have had personal contact or connections with Jesus. It stands to reason with me that many of them could easily bring words of knowledge and blessings to the group when they met, especially after receiving the Holy Spirit which would easily been an expectation they had from Jesus. As time passed and those personally connected with Jesus died, I imagine that church services began to become more like story telling events to teach history, thus preachers standing in front of a quiet audience. This is an oversimplification I know.

I also know that in my searching of churches for one that I would call home I experienced varied styles of worship. My question was "If God is still alive, where is He in a church service?" It was that search that finally lead me to Jan Coverstone and his understanding and connection with God that is very uncommon in American churches today. This style church is not a primitive, oppressive, antiquated church; we are a body of believers seeking and knowing a real connection with the Father. We are not told what to feel and say. We are freed to let the Holy Spirit work through each of us uniquely and to hear from our Father. This concept is foreign and confusing to many people because it is far from the "norm" in churches today. Mr. Coverstone is our pastor and he does bring us a message (sermon). I am a skeptical, questioning, independent, type A personality who will not stand for being "bossed around." We are in no way a cult. We have our own lives, families, jobs, and homes. And church is not for show or entertainment; although sometime God and the Holy Spirit can be very entertaining. I cannot imagine going back to a common church again.

Next let's think about and discuss the Vocal Gifts.

So I would like you to explore in your mind and within your study group possibilities of God / Holy Spirit lead church styles in contrast to the "normal" church you may be used to. Here are some comments by the author about the church service.

Tongues are a personal expression of prayer, intercession and praise to God. When guided by or anointed by the Holy Spirit the vocalization of a tongue and the interpretation thereof is equal to a prophecy given in the known language of the assembled believers. Paul admonishes to let everything be done decently and in order. The whole order of service is to build or edify the believer and to honor and worship the Lord. Not only are all things to be done for edification but each one should bring something to the meeting. The church was not meant to be a spectator experience, where you go to sit quietly and observe what is going on. It is to be a dynamic interaction from all the believers to each other and to the Lord. What I see in Paul's teaching is a more personal involvement.

1. How would you see a church service of this nature?

_____

_____

_____

_____

2. This section of text from this chapter questions the need for prophecy: Eight times Paul spoke of prophecy or prophesying in the fourteenth chapter of First Corinthians. He said to desire spirituals but especially prophecy and again to desire earnestly to prophesy. Why is it that so little of this is happening in the body of Christ? It is to build up the church when assembled and to build up individuals when it is done one on one. Is there any who does not need building up or made stronger? What are your thoughts on this idea?

_____

_____

_____

_____

Paul wrote that we could all prophesy one by one that all may learn and all may be encouraged. Prophecy is to edify, exhort and comfort. I want to encourage every reader to make an effort to edify, exhort and comfort. If you are willing to be used, the scripture says all can prophesy.

3. Have you ever heard anyone speak prophetically? _____

4. What can you do to gain a personal understanding of this spiritual?

_____

_____

_____

_____

5. In the text of the book we read this example: If I went to visit my dad, sat and spoke about him and expressed my love for him and never gave him the opportunity to say a word you might think that is strange and a little weird. If I did that once a week for years you might think there was something seriously wrong with me. Why would I never give my dad a chance to talk when we met together? That is far from the normal aspects of a relationship. Would I be content in that relationship? Would my dad be content in that relationship? If those questions made you stop and think then so should the next question. Why do we do this to our Heavenly Father when we gather at 'church'? Do you think He is satisfied with that expression of our relationship with Him? What are your feelings and comments on this idea?

_____

_____

_____

_____

_____

Think about tongues along with the interpretation or prophecy being a loving communication from our Heavenly Father. I believe our Heavenly Father desires to speak with us thousands of times more than our earthly parent desires to talk when we visit. Yield to the leading of the Holy Spirit and be that willing vessel. I do not want to miss what my Father has to say and I desire an intimate relationship with Him. I believe the Father absolutely desires to communicate with His children through the spirituals every time the church comes together.

What are we going to do to allow our Father to speak to us?

6. How do you think communication in possible from God? What conditions might our Father talk to us in?

_____

_____

_____

_____

_____

Paul took time to explain the spirituals in three chapters of First Corinthians. Obviously the church at Corinth needed the teaching but in the wisdom of the Holy Spirit it was also written for our learning and understanding. Little more than a casual mention of the other spirituals is noted with the emphasis being on tongues, the interpretation of a tongue and prophecy along with admonitions to be decent and orderly and seek to edify the church. The argument could be made that the church at Corinth was misusing the gifts and that is true. That does not negate the fact these chapters are a part of the Bible and are to guide our use of the spirituals also. I believe there is an importance to these chapters which has either been ignored or thrown out of the churches today.

7. What thoughts do you have as to reasons we should not ignore the spirituals of tongues and prophecy?

_____

_____

_____

_____

Ch. 7 The Ministry of Tongues

First let's remind ourselves of the information presented in Ch. 7.

Tongues are a language the _____ has never learned; it is imparted to our _____ by the Holy Spirit. Our personal _____ flows from our spirit, a gift given to us by the Holy Spirit for our use in communicating with and praising _____.

Tongues are to edify ourselves. Tongues is a _____ source to help overcome _____, build _____ and _____, and promote _____.
Praying from your spirit allows your _____ to affect the _____ world in ways we may only imagine.

Praying in the spirit may be building the _____ and the upkeep in your life and ministry.

Praying in the spirit is a builder of _____.

Praying in the spirit also can help us to build our _____ and dedication when praying for others, especially Christians I have never met.

When Paul wrote about speaking _____ or taking what is known in the Spirit realm and bringing that revelation into the physical or _____ realm he is talking about part of the outworking of the variety of tongues. The different kinds of tongues as a spiritual manifestation take on many forms or expressions.

When I pray in the spirit for myself I _____ to converse with God and begin of my own desire. When praying in tongues for different reasons I will be _____ by the Holy Spirit.

Praying in tongues is one part of living by _____ and not by _____. The whole Christian experience is a blending of the _____ and natural.

The different kinds of tongues are for _____ purposes. The various kinds of tongues are for much more than our personal needs. They are to minister to the _____ of Christ as well as magnify God.

Praying in tongues is for spiritual battles

Battles are won or _____ by our sensitivity to the urging of the Holy Spirit to _____ in the Spirit. The New Testament teaches us we are to pray. We are to _____ for those in authority in the world system. We are to _____ for those who watch over us. We are to continue to persevere in _____ and supplication for all saints.

Tongues may be for intercession

Another way the "different kinds of tongues" will function is through individual _____ for someone. My prayer in tongues for a person will vary and at times be totally different from what I usually pray.

Tongues for proclaiming and declaration

There are times when I begin to pray in the Spirit and the utterance seems to have a supernatural _____. It becomes stronger, vibrant, and full of spiritual life with the presence of the Lord magnified. I believe that the boldness carries a proclamative authority bringing a _____ from the _____ of God and the _____ of God to meet the needs of the saints gathered together.

I was led to make a declaration. It was the _____
declaration which actually set in motion events and
circumstances to bring alignment to the _____ and _____
of God. There have been other times when I felt or sensed I was
making a declaration but none compare to the magnitude of
going to the mat.

Tongues for rebuking the enemy

Tongues may bring a spiritual _____ or a commanding
of the enemy's spiritual forces to _____ our presence. The
tone and the emotion of _____ or
_____ is present when rebuking in tongues. This is an
inner awareness of the purpose of this particular tongue.

Tongues to magnify and praise

Praise and _____ is another variety of "different
kinds of tongues". There are occasions when someone will sing
in the Spirit under the anointing which ushers in a peace and
_____ of the Lord which ministers and draws all who
hear closer to the Lord.

Tongues to renew and strengthen

I have heard someone pray or speak in tongues and knew in my
spirit it was imparting _____ to my being.

Tongues open windows for other spirituals

Praying in tongues may also be the springboard for other
spirituals to be _____. Praying in the Spirit can
result in receiving dreams and _____ or having another
spiritual come along side to aide in some way.

I have read of someone speaking in a tongue which was unknown to them but the hearers understood what was being spoken. They were _____ the glory and good news of Christ Jesus to someone who had not heard the _____.

Tongues as a message for the church

Another aspect is the vocal utterance in a church to minister, intercede or receive _____.

The anointing or leading of the Holy Spirit may change a normal tongue language into another to serve His purpose. You and I cannot make the change from our normal prayer language, only the _____ _____ can bring about the various kinds of _____ and their varied aspects of ministry. They are used as ministry _____ to further the work of the Holy Spirit.

Next let's think about and discuss the Ministry of Tongues.

1. Our prayer language tongue is given to us with the freedom to pray to God as we are led. Other Tongues come through us as they are given to us, usually in a language other than our prayer language. Who determines what we say in our use of Tongues?

_____

_____

2. Praying in the spirit causes powerful and dynamic changes which influence hearts as well as circumstances. Tongues improve lives and ministries from the very foundations. Discuss the variety of positive effects that the Holy Spirit can bring about in people's lives by praying in the spirit.

_____

_____

_____

_____

_____

3. Beyond our personal needs, tongues are given for a variety of ministry purposes. They minister to the body and magnify God. They equip us for warfare thru worship. Do you see value in the different purposes the Holy Spirit uses for tongues? Discuss the different types of tongues and how their manifestation can be of benefit.

_____

_____

_____

_____

_____

4. The use of tongues has been determined to be outdated and useless for today's world by many religious leaders. Do you agree with that mindset? What harm can result from the use of tongues now? Why would Christians be instructed to avoid speaking in tongues?

_____

_____

_____

5. How many of the different kinds of tongues do you use in your walk with the Lord? _____

6. Do you desire to open your heart for all the different kinds of tongues? _____

Ch. 8 The Interpretation of Tongues

First let's remind ourselves of the information presented in Ch. 8.

The interpretation of tongues is not a translation but a way of conveying the meaning of tongues. This is usually taught as tongues and the interpretation of tongues as equal to prophesy when it occurs in a church meeting. I believe this occurs also in other settings. Each of the different kinds of tongues may be interpreted when the Holy Spirit allows or brings the interpretation. Sometimes this is revealed to bring understanding into a person's life, insight into a raging war, or the reason for intercessory prayer.

Next let's think about and discuss the Interpretation of Tongues.

1. What is the purpose of interpreting a Tongue? Why would we want an interpretation if it is a mystery language only for God?

_____

_____

_____

2. Where does the understanding for the interpretation come from?

_____

3. Who is qualified to provide an interpretation?

_____

4. When giving an interpretation must it be exactly word for word perfect?

_____

_____

Ch. 9 All May Prophesy

First let's remind ourselves of the information presented in Ch. 9.

"For you can _____ prophesy one by one, that all may
_____ and all may be _____. And the
_____ of the prophets are subject to the prophets."
(1 Cor. 14:31, 32) _____ is to edify, comfort and exhort.

Prophecy is one of the nine _____ or gifts of
the Holy Spirit. It is also listed among the grace or *Charis*
_____ mentioned in Romans chapter twelve.

Prophecy is to speak by _____ intervention or influence
to bring forth the mind of the _____ into a situation. Is
_____ which carries a Word of Knowledge or a Word
of Wisdom different from a prophecy which does carry any
other gift with the speaking forth? _____,
encouragement and speaking to _____ may or may not be
prophecy. If the _____ guidance is upon the
_____ it is prophecy.

The last part of the sentence in Revelation nineteen and verse
ten is written this way: "For the _____ of Jesus is
the spirit of _____." The Word of God or the Bible
has many prophecies and Jesus is the _____ made
_____. When we share Jesus or the Bible the
_____ of prophecy is present. This seems to indicate a
variety of levels or _____ of
prophecy. Prophecy may not be easy to define and categorize
but it should always _____ us _____ to the Lord and
_____ Word.

When sharing from the Bible with the Holy Spirit's _____ the words are not just the *logos* _____ word they become *rhema* or _____ giving words. This would be a _____ declaration.

When _____ read the Bible and _____ the promises written therein it is a form of _____ proclamation. I am pro-claiming the _____ as my own.

_____ as a spiritual is to bring forth words from the _____ of the Lord into a person or a gathering of people. They are to _____, _____ and _____.

When a prophecy carries another _____ with it such as a Word of Wisdom showing the _____ or action to be taken it may be considered a _____ prophecy.

Prophecy as a grace _____ may be edifying, exhorting or comforting and may be a blend of the Word of _____ and also from an individual's _____ or mind. When taking the Sword of the _____ which is the Word (rhema) of God it is a tool of _____. What is spoken as rhema carries life, _____ and _____.

_____ is listed as a grace _____ and may also be prophetic. Prophecy is a _____ to be used to change the _____, atmosphere and spiritual _____ in the territory in which we live.

Next let's think about and discuss the chapter All May Prophesy.

Prophecy is to edify, comfort and exhort. With so many wounded people on the planet, prophecy is needed now more than ever. Who is not lightened or their burdens lifted by an encouraging comment. Prophecy is one of the nine spirituals or gifts of the Holy Spirit. It is also listed among the grace or *Charis* gifts mentioned in Romans chapter twelve. I believe prophecy may be two separate gifts or have two manifestations. One is a spiritual under the power and anointing of the Holy Spirit to speak forth a message from the throne room of the Father. I also believe it is a grace gift where one grows in ministry to edify, exhort and encourage others. Both are needed. One may be used more in private settings and the spiritual may be used more in corporate or church service settings. It may be used by an individual to speak to another with the full anointing and power of the Holy Spirit.

1. Why do you think that our Father God and the Holy Spirit would feel the need to both give the same type of gift to us? Do you think they had the same purpose in mind? _____

_____

_____

_____

_____

2. How important do you feel it is to God and the Holy Spirit that we encourage and comfort each other? Do you believe that would only encompass our friends and family or would they desire us to use our prophetic giftings to people outside our usual circle? How can we tell that? _____

_____

_____

_____

_____

"For you can all prophesy one by one, that all may learn and all may be encouraged."

3. If God and the Holy Spirit want all to prophesy, do you think they would make it a difficult thing to do? What do you think is the key to being able to edify, comfort, and exhort a fellow human being?

_____

_____

4. Why would God and the Holy Spirit feel it is the best idea for all to be able to prophesy? What might happen to someone if only a select few may prophesy and none of them were available in someone's time of need?

_____

_____

_____

_____

_____

Ch. 10 Prophecy

First let's remind ourselves of the information presented in Ch. 10.

Prophecy is *rhema.* It is the _____ life giving _____.
Logos is the _____ word. The Greeks used rhema to
mean _____ or what was spoken. In Eph 6:17 we
are to take the _____ of the _____ which is the
word (Rhema) of God. The sword works when it is spoken as
Jesus used rhema by quoting from the _____ of God when
tempted by Satan.

Prophecy may have an element of personal
_____. Paul wrote to Timothy
about stirring up the gift and to not neglect the _____ in him
which was given by _____. Timothy had a
responsibility to _____, maintain and _____ up what was
given to him. Paul also wrote in First Thessalonians chapter five
to not _____ the Spirit and _____ _____
prophesyings. Prophecy may be for _____ or in the
_____ and we must open our hearts to _____
and take _____ if necessary.

Prophecy is not usually a _____ answer. However, a
prophecy may _____ a truth to the one receiving the
prophecy. It is more encouraging to be faithful and by being
faithful events occur. There is usually a personal
_____ to _____ in
the fulfilling or completion of a _____. There is also
the element of _____. A prophecy may _____ you and
enable you to _____ as the Lord desires. Because a prophecy
doesn't happen overnight does not mean it will not happen or
come true.

Next let's think about and discuss the chapter Prophecy.

1. Are we responsible for our obedience to the teaching of the Word of God? If we are, and I believe we are, then we also have a responsibility to allow the gifts to operate and function in our lives. Not only do we have a responsibility to seek the gifts and especially to keep on prophesying. We should know that the heart of the Father and our Lord is to be able to love others through the operation of the gifts in our lives. Are we responsible for developing our gifts including using prophecy?

_____

_____

_____

_____

_____

Prophecy and prophesying are light to a darkened spiritual world and to us individually. When the light of the Lord's word and His love flows into a person receiving prophecy and their face begins to shine and you see a spark in their eyes it is assurance that the love of the Father has reached into their lives. Prophesying may bring healing to a person in a variety of ways. Prophecies may help aid in your warfare as Paul wrote to Timothy. He also wrote so Timothy would stir up the gift in him which was given by prophecy and the laying on of hands. Paul wrote those words to Timothy because prophecy was a vital functioning gift giving encouragement to the young pastor. We need this gift of prophecy to function with the power of the Holy Spirit to edify, exhort and comfort. It is our responsibility to yield ourselves as willing vessels.

2. Is it important to continue to prophesy? What reasons do you believe encourage you to step up to your responsibility and learn more about prophecy and prophesy more?

_____

_____

_____

_____

_____

3. I believe I am to share about prophecy as part of my calling and also because of the vision. I hesitate to share this because even though I have come to believe in the experiences I have as long as they do not violate the word of God, a part of me questions why God would choose me. And, Gabriel giving me a sword sounds pretty farfetched. On the other hand I am doing what I know I must do and that is to do everything I am able to do to bring prophecy to a more active role in the body of Christ. What is our personal responsibility when a prophecy is given to us?

_____

_____

_____

_____

_____

4. Prophecy may take time to reach fruition in our lives. How should we respond when someone responds to a prophecy negatively, like saying that can never happen or it's been a week and it didn't come true?

_____

_____

_____

Prophecy will come again into prominence as the Holy Spirit ignites a passion in our spirits which will not be extinguished by the teaching of man or the attacks of the demonic realm. It is a vital tool to nurture the Bride of Christ in preparation of the Lord's return. It is to be a healing balm for the wounded, it is to be a flame to ignite passions which have grown cold from by the rejection of the world, it is to reveal the secrets of the heart to revel in the worship of the Lord, and prophesying will open the hearts for healing of many Christians who have suffered deep spiritual wounds at the hands and the words of their brothers and sisters in Christ.

5. Have you noticed any tendencies in people today to make you think that prophecy will soon have a strong influence again?

_____

_____

_____

_____

Ch. 11 Revelation Gifts

First let's remind ourselves of the information presented in Ch. 11.

The revelation gifts are the discerning of _____, the word of _____, and the word of _____. These are _____ manifestations in that all require a revelation and insight from the _____ _____ which is beyond the knowledge or insight from our _____ understanding, intelligence, or the natural ability of the soul.

_____ of spirits is exactly what is implied; it is the ability to discern the spiritual _____ of angels, demons or the spirits of men. It is _____ the gift of discernment whereby any _____ of judgment may be issued against a person or situation. Now, sometimes the Holy Spirit might reveal the cause of a situation but that would be a word of knowledge.

The discerning of _____ may operate or function through many avenues of expression. One may perceive an _____ of sulfur or rotting garbage and know there is an unclean spirit involved. Another may see a _____ or a picture flash through their mind revealing the spirit involved. _____ is another way the gift may function; seeing a darkness is indicative of an evil spirit. It may function with a sense or _____ which could be a person's spirit being prompted to be _____ of spiritual forces at work. The Holy Spirit uses varied ways to _____ to a person what is transpiring in the spirit world. Another way might be a vision or _____ or even a night vision or _____. For others it is an opening of _____ eyes and they see what is in the spirit world. Regardless of the method, it is the Holy Spirit making _____ what spirit is involved.

Seeing into the spiritual realm _____ the plan, intent and even the appearance of angelic or demonic _____. What is seen is revealed by the _____ _____. There are a variety of classes of spirits as Paul wrote in Ephesians chapter six and verse twelve: "For we do not wrestle against flesh and blood, but against _____, against _____, against the _____ of the darkness of this age, against spiritual _____ of wickedness in the heavenly places."

A _____ of knowledge is a small piece of the _____ of the Lord given by the Holy Spirit. It is a supernatural _____ into a situation, circumstance or even events in a person's life. It is something which is not known by _____ understanding.

A _____ of wisdom may be the _____ taken based upon the word of knowledge. _____may be given by a word of wisdom which is not preceded by a word of knowledge.

The word of _____ and the word of _____ often come side by side to work _____. He then _____ a word of wisdom with instructions on what to do with the word of knowledge

Discerning of Spirits is a _____ power to _____, know or see into the realm of _____ and their activities. It may work hand in hand with a word of knowledge or a word of wisdom to have a supernatural revelation of the enemy's plans and purpose and how to war against those plans or purposes. It is not the natural discernment which comes by growth and maturity as mentioned in Hebrews 5:12.

A word of Knowledge is a _____ of knowledge not known by natural avenues. It may concern the divine _____ of God. It may be facts which when known give an insight otherwise unknown. A word of knowledge may stand alone or may work in conjunction with Discerning of Spirits or a Word of Wisdom.

A Word of Wisdom gives _____ or direction for _____ the will of God. It may give personal understanding as to a course of action either for an individual or a church. Again it may function alone but also works with a Word of Knowledge and Discerning of Spirits.

Next let's think about and discuss the Revelation Gifts.

Discerning of Spirits is a revealing of the spiritual forces at work in a person, place or events. The gift may operate so we command the evil spirits to leave. It may operate with a word of knowledge or a word of wisdom so we pray, proclaim and declare freedom from oppressing spirits in a person's life or a situation.

A word of knowledge is a small piece of God's knowledge revealed to us by the Holy Spirit to have us pray for a person or situation. It may be a revealing of the plan and purposes of the Lord concerning an area of our lives or someone else's life. It is factual and is information which we may pray about and discern what our response should be to what is revealed.

A word of wisdom may lead us to know what we action we should pursue concerning a word of knowledge or discerning of spirits. A word of wisdom may reveal divine direction. It may also reveal the plan of the Lord for an individual or a fellowship.

1. The Holy Spirit reveals information as He determines necessary to help in each particular situation. Would not it be more helpful to always give us words of knowledge and wisdom with spiritual discernment? Think about and provide examples of reasons why the Holy Spirit might choose to not give added information.

_____

_____

_____

_____

_____

2. We should all desire all the gifts given by the Trinity. Discerning of Spirits, words of knowledge and words of wisdom are gifts most people would say they would desire to get. What character aspects might the Holy Spirit be considering when revealing these gifts to his body? Why might He choose not to reveal particulars to a person? How can we better prepare ourselves to be used by the Holy Spirit?

_____

_____

_____

_____

_____

_____

_____

_____

_____

3. Peter received a word of knowledge in the fifth chapter of Acts. What other gifts functioned through Peter in this chapter?

_____

_____

_____

_____

_____

4. The idea of tongues and prophecy is ignored or thrown out in many churches today. Would it make sense to throw out the revelation gifts of the Holy Spirit as well? Could there be an argument for choosing to continue accepting only select gifts?

_____

_____

_____

_____

_____

ACTIVATION EXERCISE: The Holy Spirit is able to reveal all truth. Ask the Holy Spirit to reveal truth about another person. (The Holy Spirit will not judge, condemn or reveal what is hurtful to someone except in rare instances. If you feel something may be harmful, pray and see how it may be done with grace and love and preferably privately).

Ch. 12 Power Gifts

First let's remind ourselves of the information presented in Ch. 12

The gift of _____, the _____ of Healings and the Working of _____ are known as _____ gifts. They each demonstrate an aspect of the power of God. _____ has executive clemency over all the _____ laws of the universe. When He suspends a natural _____ it allows for a miracle or _____ to take place.

The _____ of Faith is difficult to identify clearly because it almost never stands alone. Faith may bring about the Working of Miracles or the Gifts of Healings.

The _____ of Miracles may best be illustrated by Jesus turning water into wine. It was not only transformed into wine but it was very good wine. Many miracles are missed because to do what seems improbable leads to the impossible happening.

The Gifts of _____ is the _____ working of the Holy Spirit to bring healing or cures to a variety of sickness. The word Gifts is plural showing there are many gifts and ways they function. The word healings is also plural showing a variety of healings. Healing may not be automatic but might occur over time and it may require _____ on the part of the person receiving.

The spirituals are the Gifts of the Holy Spirit. As part of the sovereign Trinity the Holy Spirit in His working may _____ many of the Gifts to bring about the desired result. As such occurs we should not be overly concerned if it was a Working of Miracles or Gifts of Healings. It is the result of His gifting that one is healed, cured, delivered or maybe all three aspects were necessary for one to be made whole. Whether it was by the Gift of Faith, the Working of Miracles or the Gifts of Healings we may not have the understanding to discern which was more predominate. It really doesn't matter. The explanation of the Spirituals is to give our finite minds a glimpse into the majestic, awesome power of the Holy Spirit. By desiring the Spirituals and seeking to allow the Lord to love others through our obedience the _____ promised to those who believe is brought into reality through the _____.

Next let's think about and discuss the Power Gifts.

1. What is the difference between having and developing faith and the supernatural impartation of Faith?

_____

_____

_____

_____

2. The missionary journeys of Paul, though anointed and sent by the church at Antioch were probably a manifestation of the Gift of Faith. He had the ability to believe God without any doubt. This Faith may be the sustaining factor when facing adverse circumstance and staying strong in the witness and perseverance to achieve the Lord's will in a person's life.

What events in Paul's life might have caused Paul to have a powerful Gift of Faith?

_____

_____

_____

3. When Daniel was put into the den of lions it was because he continued his daily ritual of prayer after the edict from the king that made it illegal to ask a petition of any god. He prayed three times daily knowing he would be thrown into the den of lions. Daniel survived a night in the midst of a large number of hungry lions. Were there reasons in Daniel's life that encouraged his Gift of Faith?

_____

_____

_____

4. The book talked about a church having difficulty with erecting a tower to launch a TV station. Why was the author able to trust his Faith and follow the divine direction given?

_____

_____

_____

5. In 1 Kings Seventeen Elijah went to a widow of Zarephath whom the Lord ordained to provide for him. He asked for a drink and then asked for a little bread. It is possible what she had saved for a last meal fed three people for years. That was faith in

the Word of the Lord and it was put into action. It might have also been a Working of Miracles combined with Faith. When her son died Elijah prayed over the child and his soul came back to him. Death is something which only the supernatural gift of Faith can conquer. The Bible tells us of examples of situations that strengthen believers' faith supernaturally. Even if we have not experienced drastic conditions, can our knowledge of other's experiences help us to accept this Gift of Faith?

_____

_____

6. The working of Miracles seems rare these days. If we do hear of a possible miracle, a special person or situation seemed to be involved. Miracles just don't seem possible for us common people. How can we overcome this feeling and believe that God has Miracles available for all believers to access?

_____

_____

_____

_____

ACTIVATION EXERCISE: The power gifts are difficult to practice; are you willing to pray over someone and believe for miracles and healing or with the faith to move a mountain. (There is a story in Let The Living Waters Flow of healing and miracles because others prayed for a young woman)

Ch. 13 Led by the Spirit

First let's remind ourselves of the information presented in Ch. 13

We walk by _____ and not by _____ and the _____ shall live by faith. We need to _____ according to the Spirit. For as many as are led by the Spirit of _____, these are the sons of _____. Over twenty five times in the New Testament are we admonished to walk in _____, _____, and to walk worthy of the _____. The word walk is referring to a lifestyle of _____.

Our relationship with the Lord is a combination of _____ and _____. There are supernatural influences upon our lives. Our lives are a combination of what is _____ and physical and what is Holy and _____. We have the _____ of God in our lives which brings about transformation from the carnal to the spiritual at _____ and continues manifesting grace throughout our lives.

We have the _____ of God and we have the _____ of the apostles in the early church recorded in the book of Acts. From these we will gain _____ of how the Holy Spirit leads by taking a look at those experiences in the book of Acts. Though some of these may not seem to be supernatural leadings they are _____ steps and the practical blends with the _____.

The first aspect is to be _____. Obedience in our lives should be primary and continuous. Obedience is the first step of a lifetime journey.

The second aspect we see is _____. Their prayer was in harmony and agreement. Prayer is a dynamic force, a catalyst to bring the supernatural into the natural and it is both a spiritual tool and the way to communicate with the Father, Son and Holy Spirit. They may not have prayed exactly the same way or with the same words but their spirits were united together for a common cause.

The third aspect is _____. We are the body of Christ; we will not survive on our own. The body functions in unity and harmony and the body does what is necessary to maintain itself.

The fourth aspect is _____. The accepting of the provision of the Lord for salvation and growing in grace and walking in the Spirit is a lifetime agreement and is to be continued for a lifetime.

The fifth aspect of being led by the Spirit is _____ and _____. The joy of the Lord is our strength. Our joy is based on the Lord and the promises of His Word. Praise from a joyful heart indicates we believe He is in control and we should believe what is written and rejoice.

The sixth aspect is _____ God. Praising God releases a spiritual breakthrough from heaven to earth. The Lord resides in the praises of His people. Praise is a powerful gift we have been given.

The seventh aspect is to be _____ and _____ when going about your daily routine. It is being sensitive in daily routines when someone is encountered who needs a manifestation of the love of God through a spiritual gift.

The eighth aspect is to have a _____
_____. They had a steadfast boldness to continue sharing about Jesus and what He does in beggar's lives even when the religious system told them not to speak about Jesus. They prayed for a boldness to speak His word.

The ninth aspect is to be _____ in the things you do and be _____ to when the Holy Spirit guides you into truth.

The tenth aspect is after this happened many more believers were _____ and the ministry _____. There was a step by step process to bring the apostles and early church to where the ministry exploded.

Number eleven is that with growth comes _____. How we handle controversy determines our progress. Sometimes we do not have to handle the conflict, but give direction to others. Because of this the word spread and the disciples multiplied.

Having others help in _____ is the twelfth aspect. Each person has a responsibility to minister to one another and to serve one another.

The thirteenth aspect of being led is becoming _____ the spirit realm may _____ in new ways while we are walking by faith.

The fourteenth aspect of being led by the Spirit is _____ what may cause concern or apprehension in you.

The fifteenth aspect is we need the _____ others. Our approval, support and acknowledging of others may be the catalyst necessary for them to grow and become all they are called to be.

The sixteenth aspect is being willing to stand and travel _____ to do the work of the Lord? We all may have a season when we have to stand or work alone.

The seventeenth aspect is that we need to be _____ enough to enlist help when necessary.

The eighteenth aspect is listening and obeying those who have spiritual _____. This was not one person in charge but a group. There is a tier of spiritual authority within the church not to rule over others but to guide and serve the body for growth.

The nineteenth aspect is that the enemy will have someone who opposes what you are doing, so be _____ for the _____ of the enemy. Some form of persecution or resistance from those we try to help may also occur. The enemy tries to keep people in spiritual darkness and will resist the attempts to bring light into their world.

The twentieth aspect is to be careful _____ to accept adulation which _____ _____. There is a world of difference between being honored as a servant and being exalted. We should learn to honor those who are worthy of honor. We should strive to be worthy of honor with humility knowing it is the Lord working in and through us.

The twenty-first aspect is just doing what _____ good. No great leading, no voice from heaven, no angel telling him to stay, not even a vision he just felt he was supposed to stay. By doing what seemed good he was in the right place at the right time.

The twenty-second aspect is sometimes _____ _____ are _____ the Holy Spirit's plans. Learning to not go where we are not led is an important lesson.

The twenty-third aspect of being led by the Spirit is to be sensitive and understand _____ and _____.

The twenty-fourth aspect of being led by the Spirit is _____ the _____ and _____ from others. Each of us will have times of distress, turmoil and trials when we need others to be there and provide what is necessary for us to be victorious.

The twenty-fifth aspect is having your spirit _____ or provoked by the Holy Spirit. Exactly what Paul felt the word doesn't say but it prompted him to action.

The twenty-sixth aspect is using _____ ground to relate to others. Being able to relate to others where they are opens many doors to minister.

The twenty-seventh aspect is do not be afraid to _____ as you minister. We should be willing to work if the Lord leads and the opportunity is there. It may be just helping someone for a few hours.

The twenty-eighth aspect is receiving _____ from the Lord. When we serve the Lord, the insight, encouragement and direction of the Holy Spirit is vital to strengthen us to continue and to know where we are and where we should be.

The twenty-ninth aspect is to continue helping others to receive the _____ of the Holy Spirit. We are never too spiritual to meet the needs of others where they are in their journey.

The thirtieth aspect is in Acts 20 and verse thirty-five "It is more blessed to _____ than to receive." Being led by the Spirit should cultivate in us the ability and desire to give. We should give more honor than we receive. We should give more grace than we receive. We should give more love than we receive. We should give more thanks than we receive.

It is a _____ of _____ with sensitivity to however the Spirit leads. It is trial and error. We will not always be in perfect alignment because we are _____ and make mistakes. We should always be _____ to be in _____ with what the Holy Spirit is striving to do. Being a _____ vessel of the Holy Spirit so the spirituals and the love of the Father may flow through us and _____ the hurting lives around us is a step by step process of growing. It begins when we develop a passion and zeal for the _____ and refuse to settle for anything less than the best the Lord has for us in our lives.

Though some may see me as a _____, I believe I am _____. I have been adopted into a family. My Father is the mighty Jehovah. He is supernatural. If there is _____ anything supernatural happening in my life I would question if I am part of the family. I am normal and the _____ and _____ of the Holy Spirit are part of the family legacy. We are to be _____ guided by love, led by the Holy Spirit and seek to have the spirituals flow through us to bring the love of God into the lives of those we are in contact with.

Next let's think about and discuss the chapter Led by the Spirit.

1. To "obey" is viewed as a negative thing in today's culture. Humans want to do whatever they want and not follow rules or leadership of another in authority over them. Actually they do not want another in authority over them. Why would the Trinity expect obedience? What would be the benefits of obedience?

_____

_____

_____

_____

_____

2. We know that praising God and praying to God and having joy and gladness in our ministering sound like great things. What really can these aspects gain for us while ministering?

_____

_____

_____

_____

3. How can a mindset of continuing our christian walk help us to be led by the Spirit? Walking in a steadfast boldness, being open and ready, being honest are similar characteristics. What can these add to our ministry?

_____

_____

_____

_____

_____

4. Why would the Spirit ask us to do something that would cause concern or apprehension in a person? How could we function for the Lord if we are uncomfortable in a situation? What must we live by to work in this scenario?

_____

_____

_____

_____

_____

5. Why would we be made aware that the enemy will most likely send an attack when we are working for the Spirit and God? Being expected to minister under this condition seems so unfair. Why does God allow attacks of the enemy?

_____

_____

_____

_____

_____

6. Several of these aspects concern working with others or alone or under another's authority or finding common ground and working alongside while ministering. How do our people skills affect our ministry?

_____

_____

_____

7. Sometimes our plans are not the Holy Spirits plans, sometimes the spirit realm may open in new ways while we minister, realizing the spirit will stir and provoke our spirit, and remembering God will encourage and guide us are all aspects that we tend to forget in our humanness. How could this happen?

_____

_____

_____

8. We walk by faith and not by sight and the just shall live by faith. For as many as are led by the Spirit of God, these are the sons of God. So how do you walk so the spirituals are a part of your life? What does that mean to you? How would that show God and the Holy Spirit to others?

_____

_____

_____

_____

_____

_____

ACTIVATION EXERCISE: How are you led by the Spirit? Share stories of the leading of the Holy Spirit to encourage and build the faith of others.

Ch. 14 Led by the Spirit: Dreams and Visions

First let's remind ourselves of the information presented in Ch. 14

The word dream occurs over one hundred times in the Old Testament.

The references of dreams in the New Testament are few but those examples have significance.

In the Greek the word used is onar and refers to the natural dream process when we sleep.

Another word used in Acts 2:17 is enupniazomai which is to dream from the root which means something seen in sleep.

Another type of vision uses the word *horama* which according to Strong's Concordance means something gazed at; a spectacle especially something supernatural or a sight (vision).

Another word is *Horasis* which only occurs twice and has a meaning of gazing upon. It also carries the meaning of an aspect which is seen externally or an internal inspired appearance.

One word in the Greek is *optasia* which means a visuality, an apparition or vision *Optasia*

When Peter fell into a trance waiting for a meal to be prepared as related in the tenth chapter of the book of Acts the word is *ekstasis*. It may also be translated astonishment.

Apokalupto: to reveal, to take off the cover; and Apokalupis: disclosure or revelation

Dreams revealed the mind of _____ to various people.

Dreams may reveal the sovereign _____ of the Lord for a person or for a nation.

Dreams and visions are also a _____ from the book of Joel which Peter quoted from in the second chapter of Acts verse seventeen. "And it shall come to pass in the last days, says God. That I will pour out My _____ on all flesh; Your sons and your daughters shall _____, Your young men shall see _____, Your old men shall dream _____."

_____ and _____ are a viable means through which the Lord and the Holy Spirit reveal the _____, the _____ and the _____ of God.

This may mean seeing something in your _____ eye or seeing something with your _____ eyes. It may be _____ or _____ and may also include seeing with your _____ eyes.

This word seems to be an _____ vision. Seeing _____ beings separates this type of vision from other descriptions of _____.

It might occur as a _____ or the result of seeing something _____.

Revelations are one of the ways the Holy Spirit guides us into _____. It is a revealing of what we might not have an _____ of or a truth in the _____ of God which is what we may _____ at that time. The _____ Spirit is marvelous in all His ways.

Paul relates the visions and revelations are how he _____ in the knowledge of Christ.

The _____ and visions listed are part of the Holy Spirits _____ in our lives. All the ways we are led by the Holy _____ may be summed up when Paul wrote to the church at Galatia admonishing them to '_____ in the Spirit'.

Next let's think about and discuss the chapter Led by the Spirit: Dreams and Visions.

1. What would be the reason that there are multiple words of origin for dreams and visions?

_____

_____

_____

_____

2. Why would it make sense for the Holy Spirit to reveal God's mind and will to people in dream / vision not just appear before us and speak?

_____

_____

_____

_____

_____

3. What are major keys to "walk in the Spirit'?

_____

_____

_____

_____

_____

4. Are you aware of mini visions you have ignored before reading this chapter?

_____

_____

_____

5. How can dreams / visions be tested to make sure they are from the Trinity and not Evil distractions?

_____

_____

_____

_____

ACTIVATION EXERCISE: Share dreams and/or visions. Ask the Holy Spirit to allow you to be more sensitive to dreams and vision and pray for one another to receive dreams and visions.

Ch. 15 Love

First let's remind ourselves of the information presented in Ch. 15

First Corinthians Thirteen is known as the love chapter. It is a divine occurrence. Paul refers to spirituals in the first two verses and sacrifice in the third verse. Everything _____ _____ as the motivating and sustaining factor has no value. The last verse in chapter twelve Paul reminds us to _____ the greater gifts and yet he would _____ a supremely excellent way. In order to _____ the greater gifts we must have _____.

Paul uses _____ here for the word _____. Though the word occurs in Greek writings it came to be used to signify _____ love and _____ love for His children. The manifestation of the spirituals should be with exceeding _____ and _____. It is the draw of the Divine love _____ in the spirituals which will lead to Christ. There is no room to brag or extoll what one has done because ____ _____ but the Holy _____ is _____ of pouring the _____ of the Father through the _____ into someone's _____. The spirituals should have the gentleness and comfort of Christ our shepherd seeking and caring for a lost lamb.

The operation of the spirituals should always be with grace not _____ or impinging on the _____ of someone. The Holy Spirit is seeking to use those who are willing to be forgotten or _____ to the _____ so the Lord may become near and dear to those who are touched with a spiritual. The world and those of the world fight against the things of God and it would be easy to _____

words and actions to _____ the flow of the Holy
Spirit. Those who fight _____ God are often the ones
who want and _____ God the most. They like Paul, do not
_____ their actions are not pleasing to the Lord even
though they may believe what they _____ is right.

The spirituals have the power to _____ the yokes of
bondage which keep people enslaved. The truth and the reality
of applied truth sets people _____. Love desires to set those
who are bound free to _____ in the _____ of our Lord.
Not only does love not rejoice in unrighteousness but when we
_____ we should have a great _____ to
seek the _____ for others.

The manifestation of the spirituals is an outward
_____ of the love of God. As such, the
spirituals should also characterize the love of God. Even though
God's love is perfect, it flows through _____ vessels so
there is also the possibility the _____ of love is
imperfect. However, if we follow the guidelines of love which
Paul wrote in this chapter, there will be less of us and more of
_____ in the expression of the spirituals.

When the Lord reigns in the millennial kingdom and in the age of
ages there will be no need for the spirituals. That which is
perfect does away with all things which are now just parts of the
whole. Until that day we have a
_____ to desire and seek after the
_____ so the love of the Father and the Love
of the Lord Jesus Christ will have an _____ of grace to
_____ into the lives of those who need what only the
_____ may provide.

The spirituals function from the heart and love of God. We should _____ with His love and seek to _____ that love to others by desiring the spirituals and pursuing love. The heart of the Father is to reach and _____ the world.

Next let's think about and discuss the chapter Love.

1. Such a simple concept: Love, the key to God's ways. Not so simple to carry out as imperfect humans. Discuss how people can botch God's connection with someone in need by being not so loving.

_____

_____

_____

_____

_____

2. Does showing God's love to others mean we must be perfect in our religious language and appearance?

_____

_____

_____

_____

_____

3. Are you willing to lay aside your inhibitions and love others through the spirituals?

_____

_____

_____

4. When God has successfully connected with a person in need, we can feel accomplished and successful. Afterward is it cool to share all about it with your friends and other church members? Why or why not?

_____

_____

_____

_____

ACTIVATION EXERCISE: This is the most important chapter in this study. Discuss ways to love one another and maybe share experiences which were not done in love.

Ch. 16 But Ye Shall Receive Power...

First let's remind ourselves of the information presented in ch 16

Christ is quoted in the first chapter of Acts as saying" But you shall receive _____ when the Holy Spirit has come upon _____: and you shall be witnesses to Me in Jerusalem, and in all Judea and Samaria and to the end of the earth." The word for power is *dunamis*. According to Strong's exhaustive concordance this is _____ working power; it is a mighty power.

With _____ power the apostles gave witness and Stephen _____ of faith and power did great _____. We know _____ did great miracles. Do we have the same power? Yes, we have the same _____ and the Holy Spirit is looking for willing vessels to yield to His leading.

This power received was _____ after the Holy Spirit came upon them. This is the pattern given in the Bible. In Ephesians chapter three and verse sixteen Paul's prayer was for us to be _____ with might in the inner man. We need the power of the Holy Spirit giving _____ spirit some dunamis. Again in Collossians we are to strengthen with _____. (1:11). In Romans Paul said _____ signs and wonders by the _____ of the _____ of God was _____ when he preached the gospel of Christ. In _____ _____ verses it is referring to the *dunamis* power or might from the Holy Spirit.

Paul wrote in First Thessalonians that the _____ was not in _____ only but in _____ and in the
_____. When he wrote the second epistle to Timothy he wrote this in Chapter one and verse seven. "For _____ has not given us a _____ of fear, but of _____ and of _____ and of a _____ mind." Paul also wrote _____ would have a form of godliness but _____ its _____. God's power works _____ us, _____us and _____ us.

_____ of the twenty-seven books of the New Testament use a form of the word _____. The mighty power of the Lord is a part of our lives in the transforming miracles which happens when we _____ the provision of Christ. The _____ is held together by the authority and power of Christ. The _____ of the gospel is with dunamis, it is with the power of the
_____.

The church _____ with the power and presence of the Holy Spirit on the _____ of Pentecost. The power of the Holy Spirit is not only for the manifestation of the spirituals but also to _____ in our daily _____, to help in overcoming the flesh, to help in understanding the Word of God and to help us know the heart and _____ of the Lord.

In the King James Version the word _____ is the translation used for both dunamis and exousia, which in the New King James Version is translated _____.
Understanding the power of the Holy Spirit is to also _____ the authority which comes from the Word of God and the Holy Spirit. To manifest this authority we also need to rely upon the Holy Spirit for _____,

_____ and understanding. We have authority over the enemy but we need to know _____ to exercise that authority. That knowledge comes _____ the Word of God and the Holy Spirit.

When Christ sent the _____ to go before Him he gave them _____ over unclean spirits and the authority to heal sickness and diseases and to tread on serpents. We are adopted into the family of God with authority and power to do what the Lord _____ us to do.

I believe another aspect of understanding power and authority from the Holy Spirit comes _____ knowing the Holy Spirit is the _____ of our inheritance. The concept is the Holy Spirit is our _____, He is our down payment of eternity and He is the pledge that God will fulfill all His promises to us.

The _____ is our earnest money; he is the escrow of our inheritance. He is the _____ that as Christ was resurrected so shall we also be resurrected. He not only abides with us, leads and guides us, bears witness with our spirits that we are the children of God, but also _____ Himself with power and authority in our lives.

Next let's think about and discuss the chapter But Ye Shall Receive Power....

1. If God is all powerful and we can ask God for his involvement in our lives and those around us, why do we need power? And often times people with power abuse it. Why would the Trinity give humans this power?

_____

_____

_____

_____

2. Having the earnest of our inheritance given to us by God allows us to live how?

_____

_____

_____

_____

3. Are you walking in the power and authority granted by the Lord Jesus Christ, the Holy Spirit and the Word of God?

_____

_____

_____

ACTIVATION EXERCISE: Pray for a sensitivity to the power and authority of the Holy Spirit. Read Paul's prayer for the Ephesians, (and us) in Ephesians 1:17-19. Where else do the scriptures admonish us to accept and utilize the power given to us?

Ch. 17 The Church and "The Church"

First let's remind ourselves of the information presented in Ch. 17

The word used in the Bible for _____ is *ekklesia*
meaning those who are called out; a religious community. The
church from a Biblical viewpoint is the _____ who have
accepted and are following Jesus Christ.

The church, or the body of Christ, should be the outward
manifestation of _____'s love and His interaction with His
children.

I believe two avenues are occurring and will continue until the
Lord returns. One, there is a _____ growing
between the church as the ekklesia and the church as a religious
or Christian institution.

The Word of God is as _____ as it is
_____. We are all called of God for a purpose
and it is _____ purpose. The church is to be a _____
for Jesus. Find where and how the Lord desires for you to
_____. We will _____ to the Lord for what
we do for him.

We are to be _____ by the Holy Spirit. We are to walk in the
_____ and not in the _____. The greater our
_____ to please the Lord the more His _____ works
in and through our lives. Those who desire to be used and to
please the Lord will receive a _____ impartation of
grace and power in these last days to make a _____
in the world.

The second occurrence I believe is happening and will continue to surge forward is the _____ of many wounded saints to an _____ participation in the _____ of Christ. I believe this is a _____ act of grace from the _____ Spirit to change the heart of the wounded.

As the Holy Spirit is _____ believers to form the body of Christ many will wander from their established traditions to _____ in the grace and sweetness of the Holy Spirit. My Father is supernatural. He is the _____ of the universe and everything in it and His Son _____ all things together by His power.

Paul wrote an interesting verse in First Corinthians chapter fourteen and verse thirty-eight. "But if anyone is _____, let him be ignorant." If any choose to _____ learn and grow in understanding of the spiritual manifestations and the grace of God for those experiences let them be _____. And some will choose to not walk with the Holy Spirit's power and will miss many _____ not only for themselves but also for and to others. The results will be a _____ of power.

One last aspect of the church which has been changing and will continue to grow is in fellowship. _____ may be socializing or sharing a meal; allowing the _____ _____ to lead the time together for mutual benefit, spiritual growth and to be strengthened; and also a deeper aspect occurs on a spiritual level between the human _____.

The gospels of Matthew, Mark, and Luke recount the events in Gethsemane. The Lord went to the garden and took Peter, James and John to be _____ to Him. An angel also came

and _____ Him. I believe Jesus in His
humanity needed to _____ from the strength of their
_____ to make it through the _____ of His
prayer until the angel strengthened Him.

It also adds a dimension to the verse from Hebrews chapter ten
and verse twenty-five which states; "...not forsaking the
_____ of ourselves together, as is the manner
of some, but _____ one another, and so much
the more as you see the Day _____." We are to
assemble and exhort both with words _____ with our spirits.

That is fellowship at the _____ human spirit
_____ and is a necessity as we see the time approaching
for the Lord's _____. We give one another strength and
_____ another's spirit by our presence.

Next let's think about and discuss The Church and "The Church".

1. What is the difference between the ekklesia and the Christian
institution?

_____

_____

_____

_____

2. Are you a spectator or participant?

_____

_____

3. Why would someone choose to not learn and grow in understanding of the spiritual manifestations and the grace of God?

_____

_____

_____

4. Do you know any who were wounded by the church? Are you actively involved in their healing?

_____

_____

5. Do you remember how the fellowship of others brought healing, peace or comfort to you?

_____

_____

6. Will you be a difference maker?

_____

_____

7. Do you have a passion to prophesy?

_____

_____

ACTIVATION EXERCISE: Assemble a list of others who have been wounded or have grown cold in their faith. Pray over the list and believe God for a manifestation of His love in their lives. Accept the challenge of each one doing something personally to love someone on that list. Sometimes your spirit will minister to them by your presence. Love is an action word; let your love and the manifestation of the Fathers love make a difference in those around you.

Answer Guide

The review section of each chapter comes directly from the text of the book <u>The Gifts, Grace, and Flow of the Holy Spirit</u>. The fill-ins for those blanks will not be listed here to save space.

While all of the questions in the "think about and discuss" sections are open for personal interpretation and comments, we are including here guidelines for answers we feel fit these topics.

I like to include thought provoking questions that do not necessarily have perfect answers to encourage deeper reasoning and understanding of how God, Jesus, and the Holy Spirit work. Often times if we do not consider the opposite view we do not know how to understand and defend the ways of the Trinity.

p a = personal answer

pipa = personal interpretation, possible answers

Chapter 1

1. pipa- doubt: I don't see how this could have happened....
faith: I believe God can reach us in our worst times...

2. God is the same yesterday, today, and tomorrow. We may not notice miracles the same with advancements of technology. Some parts of miracles can be explained away, but the occurrence as a whole cannot be.

3. p a-God does amazing works; sometimes it is personal as my story is, sometimes it is in the ekklesia and sometimes in a nation. Why does God choose to move the way He does is a question we may not have the answers for on this side of heaven. It may be related to the call on a person's life. It may involve how a person's testimony will affect others. And, it may be for reasons which we do not understand.

4. pipa- no. hearing that story would not change my feelings.
yes- others testimonies make it easier to believe in God. I may have
_____ if I had experienced God this strongly.

Chapter 2

1. Jesus

2. John baptizes us into Christ so we are saved. The Holy Spirit baptizes with fire to give us power to work for God.

3. As a sign of Jesus' identity as the Messiah and also Christ did not begin His Ministry until He received the Holy Spirit. Do we need to follow this example?

4. All of us who are willing to ask

5. If you are thirsty you desire something missing inside you. If you accept what the HS has to offer then it can, in turn, flow back out of you. Thus you have become a missionary for the Holy Spirit to prophesy into other's lives, as well as and comfort or encourage. The Holy Spirit satisfies a thirst which nothing else has the power to satisfy.

6. To have comfort and God's promise is a good feeling. The comforter is also one called to walk with us in the same manner as Christ walked with His disciples. If others have given negative information about the HS you might be uncomfortable with this idea. You may feel like you would be controlled or restricted in life.

7. To allow the spiritual gifts to function to bring the Father's love into another's life; to have a greater boldness to witness.

8. They would not have been effective for the Kingdom of God. Also Pentecost events would not have occurred, which many witnessed. History of Christianity would have been different.

9. Dramatic noticeable event witnessed to many. Those in the upper room accepted baptism without fear because not alone. It was so significant and powerful that because the Holy Spirit came as He did many were added to God's kingdom that day.

10. Obvious something was happening by a higher power. Made believable. Attracted attention to them to witness. The Holy Spirit enabled them to speak in a language they never learned.

11. God

12. Proves desire. Teaches patience. Allows for clear mind. It was promised by John the Baptist and Jesus and came on the day of Pentecost. The early church believes it was important and so should we.

13. p a Hopefully we would all respond to the anointing in whatever way that may be.

14. Positive. We can all use help, esp. divine. Absolutely essential.

15. Believers would allow the HS to work thru them and live more supernaturally and Earth would feel more like Heaven. Less control by Satan. His kingdom rule and presence would reign.

Chapter 3

1. The rushing wind was the HS breath. The tongues of fire proved this was of God. And the Tongues spoken by the believers were languages of the crowd to witness to them.

2. As I don't find scripture that says this should change, I see no reason this should not still be normal today. The church is still in operation; do you think if God wanted something to change He would have another event similar to Pentecost to occur.

3. So our work for God can be more effective. By praying and being directed by the Trinity. So the love of the Father would manifest itself from us as His ambassadors into another's life.

4. Other people of influence who make up convincing arguments. People are lazy and do the least they need to for anything including their eternity. The doctrine or teaching of many denominations prohibit or teach against the teaching presented here.

5. p a Answers can generate group discussions.

Chapter 4

1. Yes, we can witness about our experience of God without the Holy Spirit. Our witness will be more powerful with the baptism of the H S. thanks to His help in our growth and being able to rely on Him to give us answers that are sought.

2. In a variety of ways the H S brings a blessing to our lives. Only misunderstanding of the baptism of the Holy Spirit would cause a believer to not want to be blessed.

3. The H S is equipping us with a greater ability to fight spiritual battles for others. Prayer in Tongues can target the points needed to be brought out to be most effective against Satan. If special information is revealed to an intercessor the HS knows they are trustworthy with this information for good.

4. The Father is more blessed by us. We are more blessed by the Father. And fellowship between believers has greater blessings. God knows our prayers in Tongues are on target.

5. p a. Answers may generate group discussions.

Chapter 5

1. God, Jesus, and the Holy Spirit each have their own roles in the Trinity. So it makes sense that each would give gifts to (those whom He has called to) be better equipped according to their roles.

2. Every gift is valuable. Some may be more specific to certain individuals by their nature and talents. Some may be more effective in various situations. All have necessary importance.

3. I believe the H S places high importance on all of the spirituals. Men of today may have decided that some are more easily faked or abused or have even experienced this and feel it is easier to eliminate the problem than teach proper usage of those spirituals. Or maybe they don't understand either.

4. The desire to see God's love flow into another's life and bless them.

Chapter 6

1. Location anywhere conducive and available for a gathering. Anytime we go to The Father we bring praise & honor. How best would you like to do that? Singing, music, dance, words of praise, prayer. And a time of worship: singing, music, dance, praise & prayer as well. Large group setting, various group and individually interactions. Time of quiet connection with God: prayer, waiting, listening. Possible messages in Tongues with interpretations, prophecy. Time of sharing of blessings. Time of a sermon or teaching, may include some questions. Communion time. Fellowship time may be prior to or after the service. May want to include food or snacks depending on group. The time designated will probably be significantly more than the 1 hr church service; easily 2 to 3hrs.

2. pipa,

3. p a

4. Seek Christians who are spirit filled and fellowship with them. Ask the H S to come into your life and experience it personally.

5. pipa, not used to hearing God. Waste of everyone's time to sit and do nothing. People would get restless. Makes sense Father would respond to child. Expected to do on personal time- unknown by most so doesn't happen.

6. Quiet, patience, supernatural ability, quiet voice in mind, through another Christian

7. Included in bible, importance and value discussed in bible, way people can be helped.

Chapter 7

1. The Holy Spirit

2. Relationships, healing, employment, government issues, weather issues, anything we deal with. Praying changes the chemistry of the body, boosts the immune system, releases anxiety and may bring peace.

3. For battling spiritual enemies that we humanly do not know how to deal with, for proclaiming changes or positions that the enemy needs put it its place about as well as impacting ourselves to realizations too, to pray for others when we do not know the situations, to praise God, to strengthen someone, to deliver a message from God for ministry work.

4. True spiritual tongues should not cause harm unless to a demonic force. Someone could claim to be speaking in tongues and be summoning demonic beings? Many ministry leaders today have little understanding about tongues and may be afraid of the unknown or possibly are off God's course on their own agenda and do not want discovered.

5. p a

6. p a

Chapter 8

1. To give us understanding of a tongue that we gave or heard. When the mystery language is a message from God he would want us to know what that message is to improve life. Tongues and interpretation equals prophecy.

2. The Holy Spirit

3. Whomever the Holy Spirit has entrusted with the message.

4. It is basically a description of the message, not said as "God said". Sometimes even pictorial descriptions are used to explain. It is an interpretation and not a translation.

Chapter 9

1. Prophecy is important to us. They may have variations in specifics but have similar purpose. It is possible to encourage, edify and comfort with our natural understanding and this ability may grow with practice. This would be the prophecy taught in Romans 12. The same words under the anointing of the Holy Spirit would carry a deeper spiritual sense and may affect a person totally differently.

2. People are here to help each other thru life, either with encouragement or a deeper message from God. Sometimes another crosses our path and we may wonder why. If we really think about what was talked about and feelings noticed we realize that we were just the stranger that person was supposed to meet that day to get them thru. By being sensitive to the Holy Spirit our words of prophecy should reach and touch those whom the Father desires to love when we are in their presence or in communication with them.

3. Prophesying seems scary because it is a fancy term we may not be used to. It is easily done by us with someone we are comfortable with and we don't even know its prophecy. Key is being willing and the desire to be used.

4. Prophecy should be part of normal human interaction, not just on rare dire occasions. Usually the person who is with you is who God or the Holy Spirit thinks is the best one for the job.

Chapter 10

1. Simply if we don't grow and improve that which should be part of our lives, whatever it may be, who will? The Holy Spirit can guide and teach us if we are active students. Our desire to love others through prophecy should override any teaching contrary to being obedient to the word of God and the leading of the Holy Spirit.

2. The Bible tells us it is. The better we are the better God can love others through us. We should always strive to do our best for God. Prophecy is a simple way to love others and to impact their lives in a positive direction with the Fathers love. Our words have the power of life to lift oppression, discouragement and disillusionment off someone's life. What a blessed privilege.

3. We should pray about a prophecy to see what God shares with us concerning what was spoken and then cooperate with the message given. In first Thessalonians we are told not to despise (think lightly of, not value properly) prophesies. The higher value we place on them and write them down and pray over them the greater the impact in our lives. We should also judge or consider what we are able to do to cooperate with the Holy Spirit in having a prophecy bring forth it is fruit in our lives.

4. We can reassure them that often prophecies do not have quick results. And negative speaking towards God's words can block them. A prophecy may be for a situation or short time or a lifetime. Praying and seeking the Lord and allowing our spirit to be led, comforted and reassured by a prophecy may help in understanding.

5. p a - People seem to be searching for spiritual answers. I have observed people becoming interested in prophecy. As the world grows darker the light of prophecy may be a powerful help to endure, overcome and be victorious. The need is already great are we willing to love others with the light of prophecy?

Chapter 11

1. Peoples personal information is not often our business. We don't need to know private information to pass along God's message to someone. Sometimes too much information might scare or make another uneasy and less receptive to what the Holy Spirit is doing in their lives.

2 Insensitivity to others, gossip, or judgmental tendencies would be unfavorable, while the Holy Spirit may be seeking discretion, kindness and acceptance when more information needs revealed. The HS would not want to jeopardize someone to give them some news. We should strive to more Christ like. We might need to be more sensitive to the Holy Spirit and His leading by asking to be shown how the Holy Spirit desires to move and accomplish. We may not have complete answers and direction but enough information to be obedient knowing our obedience will allow the Holy Spirit to move.

3. Word of wisdom, healing, Sign and wonders were done (which may be a combination of healings), faith and the working of miracles.

4. It would only make sense if the Bible, the Word of God, would say to do so because those gifts have been discontinued. There has been found no statement of this direction. These gifts could be imitated or said to be from a person's understanding and not a spiritual manifestation from the Holy Spirit so they might be seen as more acceptable in that sense.

Chapter 12

1. Having and developing our faith is an ongoing process we gain with experiences and understanding. The Gift of Faith is a supernatural impartation from the Holy Spirit to enable us do God's work. This impartation would shake the spirit world in a way far beyond the scope of our normal daily faith.

2. Saul's encounter with Jesus on the road to Damascus where he was blinded but not killed. Then Ananias prayed over him to be filled with the Holy Spirit. Realizing he was chosen would be a powerful introduction to Gift of Faith. He also had dreams, revelations and journeys to the third heavens and spent time alone where the Lord manifested Himself and taught Paul.

3. Daniel knew he had been given interpretations to the King's dreams and his life had been spared this far. He was probably standing close when his friends went into the furnace. He had seen many visions and talked with Gabriel.

4. The author had experience and understanding of the prompting of the Holy Spirit. He believed in God's ways. To not be concerned about the obstacle on the way but to pray not for the final outcome but to pray for the operational needs because by faith he knew it would be a reality.

5. I believe if we are smart we will accept and gain from other's experiences or else we shall have to all go through all tragedies to grow in our ability to accept this Gift of Faith. We have been given the ability to communicate, shouldn't we use it?

6. We need to believe that we are all special in God's eyes and He wants to treat us all equally well. Encouraging others to believe this about themselves is a positive message all need to share. God is no respecter of persons. He never changes. Because He never changes we should not allow our culture, our church or anything in our lives to change our viewpoint of a never changing Father and Lord.

Chapter 13

1. Being a Christian is working for God and doing God's will. If we are not obedient then we are not in God's will. If the Holy Spirit cannot trust us to follow his plan and guidance then he cannot use us. The more obedient we are, the more we can be used and the more that can be revealed to us as necessary. Do we really desire for God's kingdom, His will, ways and authority to be manifested through our lives and our communities? What must we change in our lives to bring it to pass?

2. Joy in the Lord is much more than just being cheery. The understanding of the Lord should bring us peace and security; this results in making us strong for the Lord; joy is our strength with which we can be more confident to work for God. Praising God brings his attention to us and releases spiritual breakthroughs from heaven; thus making us more effective in our ministry. People will more easily have faith in what God can do for them if our prayers are done in more positive tone. Even in our imperfections the Lord sees the heart and His grace may flow through our imperfections.

3. If we believe that our ministry for God is forever we will be always finding a way to grow and improve for God and seeking opportunities to do His Will. We will more readily notice those whom need our time and prayers. We won't want to deceive others or feel like quitting or avoiding situations in which we may be needed to work. This will add credibility and can also increase our quality of ministry as we grow in service.

4. Our faith and trust in God should allow us to do things for God that we may be unsure about. God works through us. It is not of our ability or works that miracles can be done through us. Our fears and apprehension should decrease as we are used more and we see the results that can happen with our obedience

5. God allows attacks to prove He is greater than their intended havoc and destruction. He warns us so we will be prepared. Life is never fair and pushing through the difficult times will strengthen us and our testimony. God never said being a Christian makes life easy and without tests, just that we have an eternal future and that we can share that hope with others.

6. How we are seen by others influences the involvement others are interested in having with us. Our effectiveness will be better if we can teamwork with others.

7. We need to remember that God will guide us through whatever it is we need to accomplish for him. Flexibility in our work is more effective and not let our agenda get in the way of seeing opportunities that change in our path.

8. pipa, Others notice whether our faith is actually real by how we deal with everyday situations. Do we freak out or remain calm? So we persevere or give up? Are we patient or expect our way immediately? Our level of faith shows outwardly.

Chapter 14

1. Dreams and visions can occur in different ways and for different purposes. The Greek had more specific words to indicate which they were talking about.

2. A way that a Word of God or other truth that we need to know about may better can be revealed to us. We can picture it and get a better sense about it; not just be told about.

3. To live, to follow, being devoted to living by the spirit takes faith and a steadfastness that is strong. Knowing the Lord wants to communicate with us should lead us to seek to see and hear all He desires to communicate with us.

4. p a

5. Ask if they are of God. Pray about them. Ask someone for help who has a greater spiritual knowledge.

Chapter 15

1. Being in a not social mood for various reasons can cause insensitivity and hurt feelings sometimes simply due to bad timing. Viewing situations from different viewpoints can cause confusion and frustration. It is easy to allow personal frustrations or disappointments to cloud our judgment and not see a complete or even a clear picture of another's need for love.

2. It seems most people are looking for someone who is open and honest to share with not bible thumper. Terminology is important to understanding, don't want to confuse someone. Love covers a multitude of sins. Do we ever love perfectly.

3. p a

4. It is a good feeling when you have witnessed and encouraged and connected with someone. Boasting about what we have done is not Godly. I do not believe Jesus went back to the disciples and told tales about what he did for everyone he met. We should share what has been done to increase another's faith or encourage and uplift others but a simple rule is to see who is receiving the attention or glory.

Chapter 16

1. When the Holy Spirit can trust us to use God's power for his Will, we can be witnesses, healers, and helpers to those around us while God is busy with many more situations. We still summon his power and Will with our prayers. We are being trusted not to abuse our positions and can expect to be dealt with unpleasantly if we do.

2. With more confidence & peace. With praising & rejoicing.

3. p a

Chapter 17

1. The ekklesia is the church, the called out ones. As such we are to be and do all in our power not only to represent Christ but also to bring His will and His ways to our communities; to allow His kingdom to come to earth. The Christian institution may be bogged down by tradition, teaching and a culture which they may believe is right but may miss much of what the Lord desires.

2. p a Do we participate in some aspects and not in others?

3. Some believe that God will give them what He wants them to have and therefore there is no reason to seek and desire the spirituals. No one receives salvation without seeking the Lord. All we do is a combination of what God does and what we do.

4. p a Are we praying for those to come into our lives?

5. p a

6. p a

7. p a

I hope that you have gained understanding of the Holy Spirit, of God's ways and desires. May you be a blessing to another each and every day. The world is in great need of Love. God's blessings to you.

-Brenda

Made in the USA
San Bernardino, CA
28 July 2020